Günter Gerngross • Herbert Puchta

PLAYWAY 4

W0210522

PUPIL'S BOOK

Helbling

Unit 1

Favourite places

1 Watch the story. Listen and write.

Max at the rodeo

What's your name? Help! Help! Great idea! No way, Max!

Let's have | sorry | My money!

2 **Listen and fill in the numbers. Read.**

(3)

Hi! I'm Erica from Canada.

My favourite place is the tree house in our garden. I often go there. I read books and listen to music on my mp3-player. Sometimes I go there with my best friend, Pat.
Find my photograph.

(2)

Hi! I'm Stuart from California.

My favourite place is the Natural History Museum in Los Angeles.
I often go there with my grandma.
I like the dinosaurs best.
Find my photograph.

(4)

Hi! I'm Neil from England.

My favourite place is Heathrow Airport in London.
I sometimes go there with my dad at weekends. I love watching the planes take off and land.
One day I want to be a pilot.
Find my photograph.

(6)

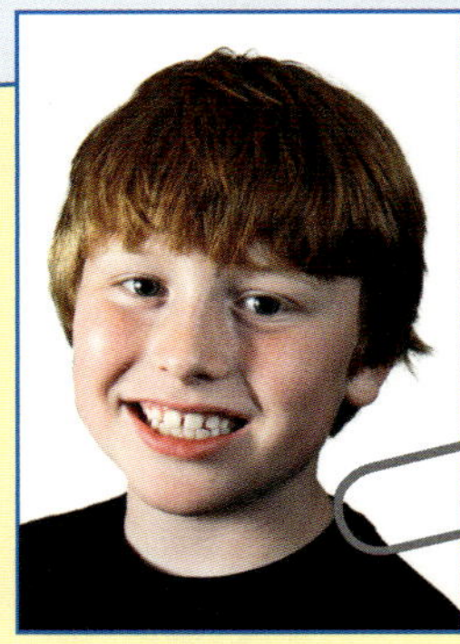

Hi! I'm Dylan from Ireland.

My favourite place is the skate park near our school.
I go there on Saturdays and Sundays.
Find my photograph.

(1)

Hi! I'm Emma from Scotland.

My favourite place is the school library. I go there every day.
I love reading.
Find my photograph.

(5)

Hi! I'm Christine from Australia.

My favourite place is the beach near our house. I often go there with my friends. We swim in the sea and build sandcastles. We sometimes find beautiful shells.
Find my photograph.

2 CD 1/3

3 Match the texts in 2 with the photographs.

3

4

6

2

7

5

4 Read. Write your own text.

My favourite place

My favourite place is the park near our house. I often play football there.

My favourite place is the swimming pool in our town. I often go there. I love swimming.

My favourite place is the trampoline in our garden. I really like it.

5 Listen. Sing the song.

Flying in a jet plane

I'm flying in a jet plane,
I'm flying fast and high.
I'm flying in a jet plane,
I'm racing through the sky.

I'm on my way to London,
with friends from near and far.
From England, Germany and Spain,
hey, in my super plane. Yeah!

I'm flying in a jet plane,
I'm flying fast and high.
I'm flying in a jet plane,
I'm racing through the sky.

I'm on my way to London,
with friends from near and far.
From Austria and Italy,
from Greece and Hungary. Yeah!

I'm flying in a jet plane,
I'm flying fast and high.
I'm flying in a jet plane,
I'm racing through the sky.

Unit 1

6 Do the quiz. Read and tick (✔). Say.

1 Which mushroom can you NOT eat?

2 Which animal doesn't live in the wood?

3 Which leaf matches this tree?

4 Which tree is not green in winter?

5 What should you do in the wood?

5 Very good!	3–4 Good!	1–2 Try again!

Family and friends

1 Listen and point.

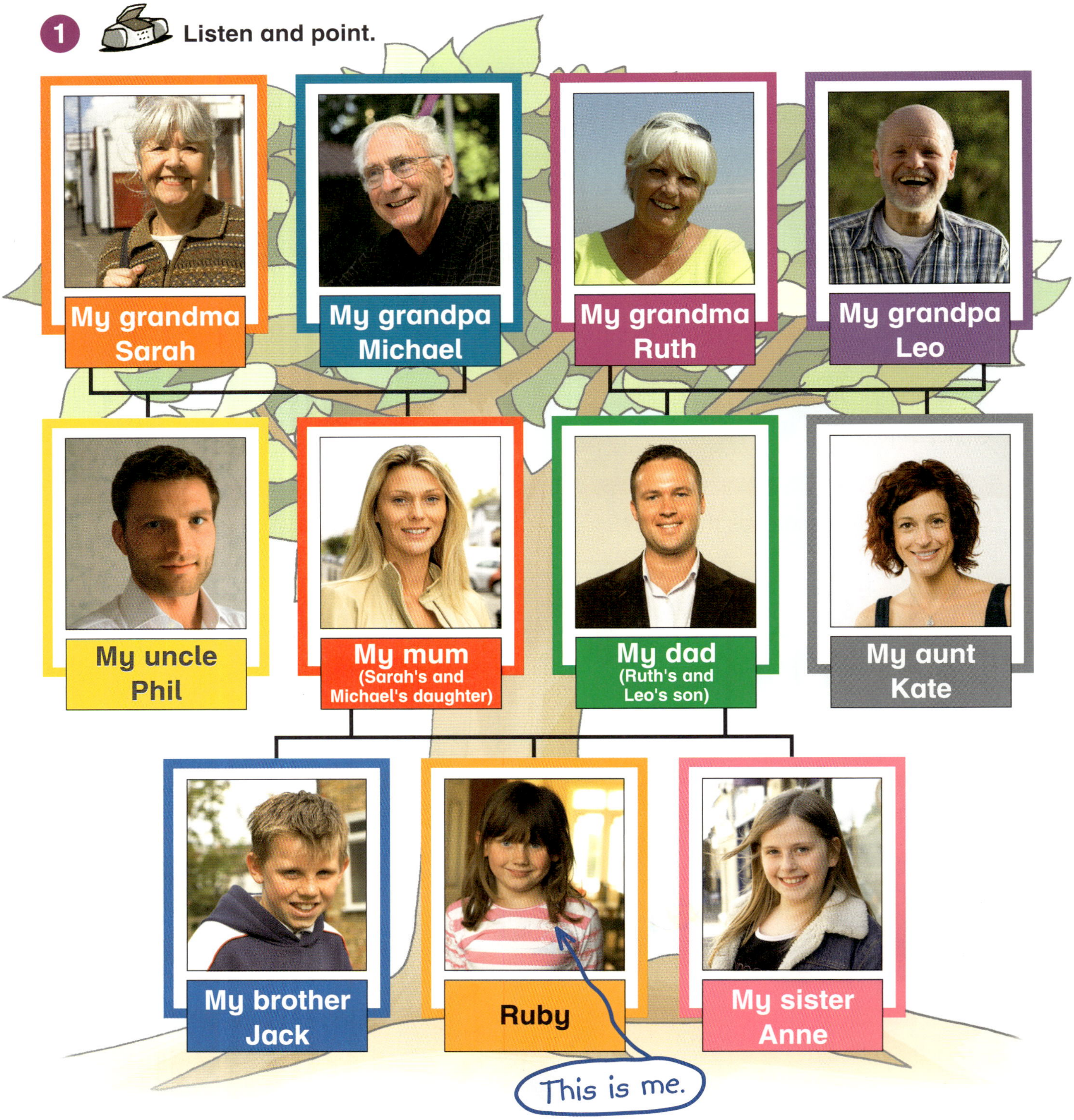

2 Look at **1** and write the names. Then ask your partner.

Who is Anne's brother? Jack

Who is Jack's uncle? Pil

Who is Kate's mum? Ruth

Who is Phil's dad? Michael

Who is Michael's son? Pil

Who is Ruth's daughter? Kate

Who is Ruby's aunt? Kate

Who is Kate's brother? Michael

1 CD 1/6

3 Listen. Find Alisha's, Brandon's, Isabel's and Ryan's family.

3 CD 1/7

4 Watch the story. Listen and write.

A letter for Lynn

She's got | What | There's a letter | That's unfair

 4 CD 1/8

What's the time? | Bad luck | Open it

5 **Read Bertram's letter to Humphrey. Draw a picture of Bertram's girlfriend. Write her name under the picture.**

6 Listen to the interviews. Tick the correct answers (✔).

Julie has got a brother. His name is
- [x] Jamie.
- [ ] Johnny.

Julie's brother is
- [ ] ten.
- [x] eleven.

He has got a
- [x] dog.
- [ ] cat.

He likes
- [ ] playing football and swimming.
- [x] swimming and skating.

He doesn't like
- [x] music.
- [ ] his sister.

Mark has got a sister. Her name is
- [ ] Hilary.
- [x] Alison.

Mark's sister is
- [ ] nine.
- [x] ten.

She has got a
- [ ] cat.
- [x] mouse.

She likes
- [x] playing football and listening to music.
- [ ] playing football and watching TV.

She doesn't like
- [ ] singing songs.
- [x] playing computer games.

7 Read. Write your own text.

My text

My name is Tom.
I'm nine years old.
I've got a brother and a sister.
His name is David
and her name is Barbara.

Unit 3

The spooky castle

1 **Look at the picture on page 14. Can you answer the questions?**

1. How many spiders are there?
2. How many bats are there?
3. How many rats are there?
4. One spider likes apples. What colour is it?
5. Two rats like chocolate. What colour are they?

6. What's the big ghost's name?
7. What's the small ghost's name?
8. Where is the big ghost's pen?
9. Where are the big ghost's in-line skates?
10. Where is the small ghost's watch?

2 **How many true sentences can you make?**
How many untrue sentences can you make?

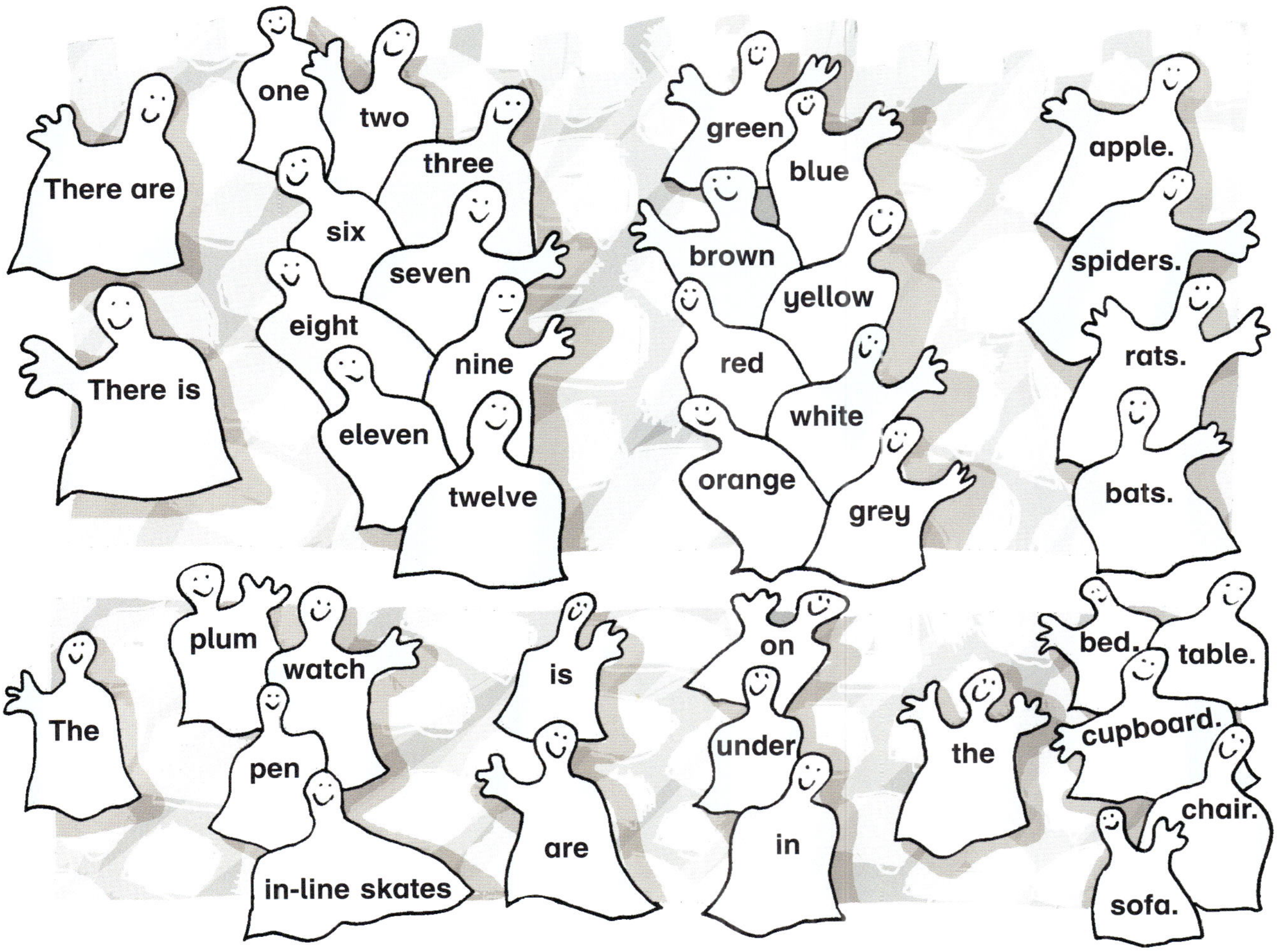

3 Watch the story. Read and write.

Ghosts

There's something cold in my bed.
Well, I'm hungry. Wake up, Danny! Don't be silly.

4 Listen and read. Find the photographs.

Culture Special

Castles in Scotland

Every summer, thousands of tourists come to Scotland. Many of them want to see the beautiful castles. One of them is Edinburgh Castle.

There are lots of lakes in Scotland. The Scottish word for lake is "loch". Loch Ness is a famous lake.

Some people say there is a monster in that lake. The monster is called Nessie. Is Nessie a fish? A dinosaur? Nobody knows.

Castle Urquhart is on Loch Ness. It is one of the oldest and biggest castles in Scotland. It is more than 800 years old.

1

2

3

4

5 Listen. Sing the song.

The spooky castle

In the middle of the wood
there's a castle dark and old,
dark and old.

There are spiders,
there are rats,
there are owls
and there are bats
in the spooky, spooky castle
in the middle of the night.

When the clock strikes twelve,
the ghosts begin to sing:
hoo hooah hoo.

There are spiders,
there are rats, …

When the clock strikes twelve,
the ghosts begin to dance:
hoo hooah hoo.

Hooah hooah hooah hoo,
hooah hooah hooah hoo
in the spooky, spooky castle
in the middle of the night.

When the clock strikes twelve,
oh yeah, they sing and dance:
hoo hooah hoo.

6 Read. Write your own text.

My text

Come to my spooky castle.
There are three ghosts.
Charlie, Archie and Ben.
There is also a big green spider.

7 How to make Halloween food: apple bites and spiders.

You need:
- a knife
- a cutting board
- an apple
- slivered almonds

1 Cut the apple like this:

2 Press the almonds in place for teeth.

You need:
- a knife
- a cutting board
- 2 round crackers
- soft cheese
- 8 pretzel sticks
- 2 raisins

1 Make a cracker sandwich.

2 Insert the eight legs.

3 Put the raisin eyes on top.

Units
1-3

Show what you can do

1 **Look, read and fill in the numbers.**

1 

2 

3 

4 

5 

6 

7 

8 

9 

10 

11 

12 

◯ beach	◯ library	◯ tree
◯ letter	◯ shells	◯ rat
◯ owl	◯ airport	◯ castle
◯ ghosts	◯ bat	◯ lake

2 Fill in the missing words.

doesn't	is	has got	brother	likes	thirteen

Sandra has got a ________________ .

His name ________________ Ben.

Sandra's brother is ________________ .

He ________________ a dog.

He ________________ playing football and cooking.

He ________________ like playing computer games.

3 Find the correct answer and fill in the numbers.

1	Are you hungry?	◯	The museum.
2	How many sisters have you got?	◯	It's Bill.
3	What's your favourite place?	◯	They're in the park.
4	Can I try, please?	◯	Two. Emma and Lucy.
5	Who is Mike's brother?	◯	Don't be silly.
6	Let's have some ice cream.	◯	Yes, they are.
7	Where are Bob and Jane?	◯	Yes, I am. Can I have a sandwich?
8	There's a ghost in my house.	◯	Yes, he is.
9	Is Paul hungry?	◯	Great idea.
10	Are Daniel and Andrew angry?	◯	Yes, of course.

Unit 4

Food and drink

1 **Listen and draw the correct faces.**

Note
I like
I don't like

2 **Talk to a partner.**

CD 1/13

3 Listen and draw the correct faces.

Note
☺ she likes
☹ she doesn't like

	Chloe	Rachel	Megan	Isabel
hamburgers				
fish and chips				
chicken and rice				
hot dogs				
pizza				

4 Test your partner.

5 Listen. Sing the song.

Luba's restaurant

Luba's is a crazy restaurant.
Luba's is the place to go.
Luba's is the place for you and me,
come here and you will see!

There is fish in your orange juice and
ice cream on your steak.
There's fruit on your pizza,
and salad on your cake!

Luba's is a crazy restaurant.
Luba's is the place to go.
Luba's is the place for you and me,
come here and you will see!

There are nuts in your tomato soup
and coffee on your pie –
and on top of your dessert
there is a fly!
Oh, no!

6 Interview four friends. Write and draw the correct faces.

	Tim				
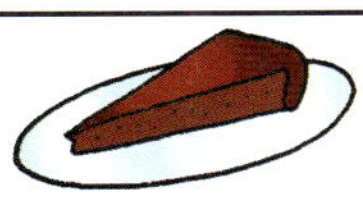					

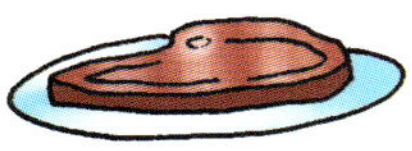					

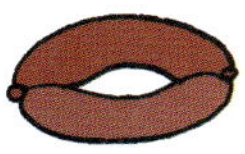					

7 Talk about your classmates.

8 Watch the story. Listen and write.

Toffees for Annabel

Can you help me | sausages | What is it?

water idea I can't help you.

9 Listen and mime. Then listen and point.

Fast food

10 Listen and fill in the numbers.

11 How to make a strawberry-banana milkshake.

You need:
- 4 cups of milk
- 1 small banana
- 1 bowl of strawberries
- 2 teaspoons of sugar
- a blender

1 Wash the strawberries.

2 Cut them into small pieces.

3 Cut up the small banana.

4 Put the milk into a blender.

5 Add the sugar, strawberries and the banana.

6 Mix everything. Yummy!

Unit 5

Birthdays

1 Listen. Say the chant.

My birthday

My birthday's not in January,
in February or March.

My birthday's not in April,
in May or in June.

It isn't in July, in August
or September.

It isn't in October
or even in November.

Remember, remember,
my birthday's in December!

2 Listen and read. Then play the guessing game.

Sandra, is your birthday in summer?

No, it isn't.

Is it in autumn?

Yes, it is.

Is it in September?

No, it isn't.

Is it in October?

Yes, it is.

1 CD 1/20–22 2 CD 1/23

3 Listen and mime. Then listen and point.

The birthday party

4 Listen and fill in the numbers.

5 Watch the story. Read and write.

Daisy's birthday

And now your present, Dad. | I want that necklace.
Blow out the candles and make a wish. | What would you like?

6 Work out the children's names. When are their birthdays?

A	B	C	D	E	F	G	H	I	J	K	L	M	N	O	P	Q	R	S	T	U	V	W	X	Y	Z
–	●	◖	▮	□	#	■	○	✱	ᗡ	◗	☺	✦	\	▲	▼	=	✚	›	ᗞ	‹	✔	☹	❤	/	✖

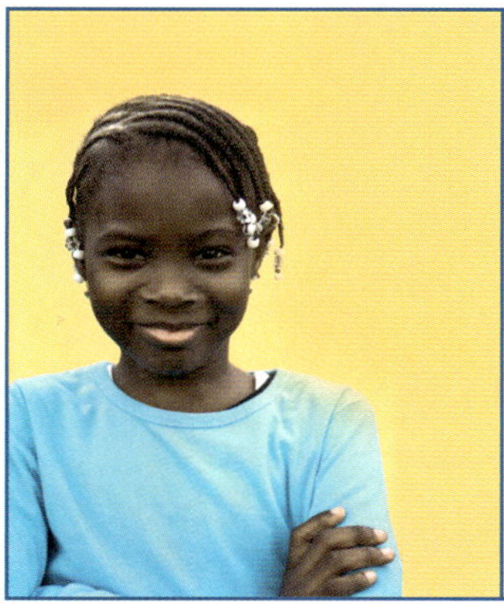

□ ✦ ✱ ☺ /

E _ _ L _

✦ ? ? ◖ ?

_ _ _ _ _

› – ✦

_ _ _

? ‹ ? /

_ _ _ _

◖ ○ ✚ ✱ ›

_ _ _ _ _

? – ? ‹ – ✚ /

_ _ _ _ _ _ _

› – ☺ ☺ /

_ _ _ _ _

? ◖ ? ? ● □ ✚

_ _ _ _ _ _ _

7 Write your own birthday month in code.

____

8 Now write a secret message.

9 Listen and read the poem.

Don't be shy

Have some pizza,
have some cheese.
Have some fish,
and have some peas.

Have some beans,
and have some steak.
Have some ice cream,
have some cake.

Have some fruit,
and have some pie.
Have some chocolate,
don't be shy!

10 Write your own poem.

Have some _______________________ ,
have some cheese.

Have some _______________________ ,
and have some peas.

Have some _______________________ ,
and have some steak.

Have some _______________________ ,
have some cake.

Have some _______________________ ,
and have some pie.

Have some _______________________ ,
don't be shy!

9 CD 1/26–27

11 Listen and read.

12 Change the dialogue and act it out.

13 Read. Write your own text.

My text

My birthday is in March.
It's on a Friday this year.

My text

My birthday was in October.
It was on a Wednesday last year.

Wild animals

1 Listen and point. Then speak.

monkey
polar bear
crocodile
lion
seal
kangaroo
elephant
shark
penguin
rattlesnake
owl
leopard
seagull
hippo
giraffe
whale

2 Look at the animals in **1**. Answer the questions.

Wild animal quiz

How many of the animals can fly?	Two.
How many of them have got four legs?	Sevin nine
How many can climb trees?	Two
How many eat other animals?	twolf
How many eat grass?	foor
How many lay eggs?	veife, siks

3 Now listen and check your answers.

4 Listen. Sing the song.

Lucy's pet

I've got a friend called Lucy.
She lives at number four.
When Lucy walks her pet,
oh yeah,
we all run to the door.

She hasn't got a hamster.
She hasn't got a cat.
She hasn't got a bear,
oh no,
she hasn't got a rat.

She hasn't got a monkey.
She hasn't got a dog.
She hasn't got a snake,
oh no,
she hasn't got a frog.

When Lucy walks her pet,
oh yeah,
the children do not smile,
because the pet she's got,
oh yeah,
is … a crocodile.

5 Watch the story. Listen and write.

Pinky the elephant

hurts lets go meets hear picks

 5 CD 2/5

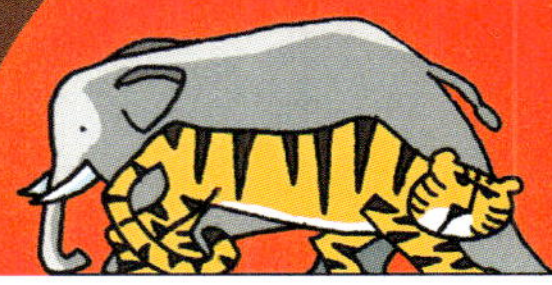

come on	drinks	Go down	family	get	Help!

6 Listen and mime. Then listen and point.

The snake

7 Listen and fill in the numbers.

6 CD 2/6 7 CD 2/7

8 Play the animal guessing game.

Has it got four legs?
Has it got two legs?

Can it fly?
Can it climb trees?
Can it swim?

Is it big?
Is it small?
Is it a …?

Does it live in …?
Does it eat fruit?
Does it eat grass?
Does it lay eggs?
Does it eat other animals?

9 Read. Write your own text.

My text

It's a bird.
It can't fly.
It can swim.
It likes cold weather.
What is it?

a penguin

My text

It has four legs.
It lives in the water.
It has a big mouth.
It eats other animals.
What is it?

a crocodile

Units 4–6

Show what you can do

1 **Look, read and fill in the numbers.**

1

2

3

4

5
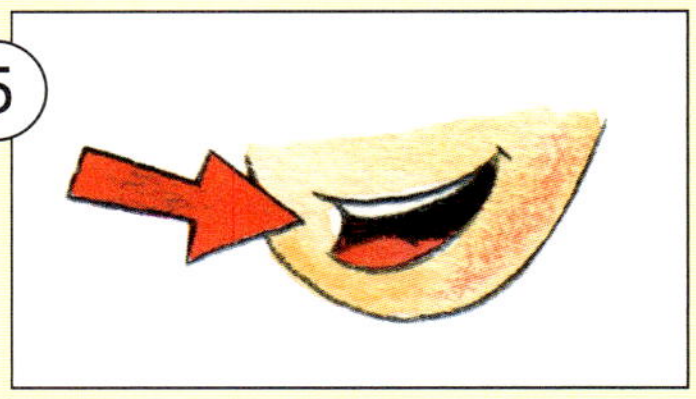

6

7

8

9

10

11

12

◯ necklace	◯ peas	◯ chicken
◯ tea	◯ candle	◯ shark
◯ kangaroo	◯ present	◯ cake
◯ monkey	◯ mouth	◯ seagull

2 Write the missing words.

__________ it got four legs?

__________ it fly?

__________ it small?

__________ it eat other animals?

3 Match.

1 How many pets have you got?	◯ No, I don't.
2 What would you like?	◯ I can.
3 Can your favourite animal fly?	◯ A necklace, please.
4 Who can bring ice cream?	◯ Yes, it can.
5 Is your birthday in winter?	◯ Two.
6 Do you like fish?	◯ No, it's in June.

4 Write the missing words.

cake	can	some	that	bring	have

 Let's __________ a birthday party for Sandra.

 Great idea. I can __________ a birthday __________.

 And I can bring __________ sandwiches.

 Who __________ bring orange juice?

 No problem. I can do __________.

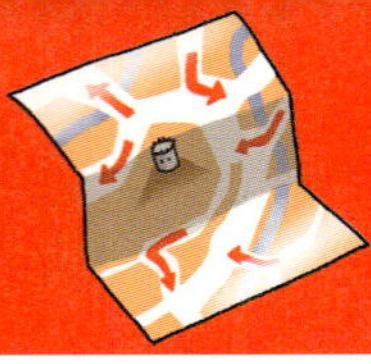

Moving about

1 **Listen and point. Then test your partner.**

Turn left.

Go straight on.

Turn right.

Go past the station.

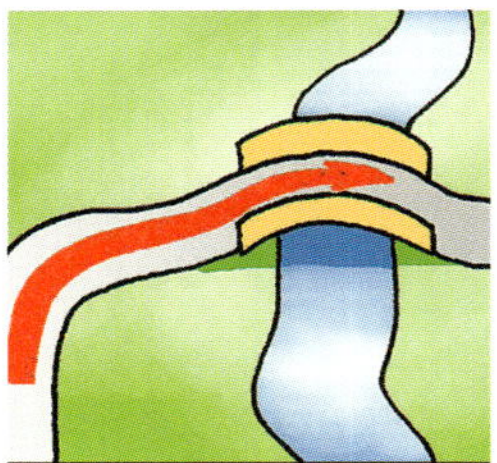

Go across the bridge.

Go through the park.

There's a big tree next to the house.

The green house is opposite the red house.

2 **Listen and fill in the numbers.**

1 post office

2 cinema

3 hospital

4 museum

5 supermarket

1 CD 2/8 2 CD 2/9

3 Listen. Say the chant. Do the actions.

Where's the cinema?

Excuse me, Monica,
where's the cinema?
Sorry, Joe.
I don't know.

Excuse me, Pamela,
where's the cinema?
Sorry, Joe.
I don't know.

Excuse me, Barbara,
where's the cinema?
Sorry, Joe.
I don't know.

Thank you, Monica.
Thank you, Barbara.
Thank you, Pamela.
I'll forget the cinema.
I'll have some tea
and watch TV.

4 Read and tick the correct text (✔).

☐ Go straight on. Go past the supermarket. Turn left. Go across the bridge. Then turn right. Go past the school and turn left. The cinema is opposite the museum.

☐ Go straight on. Go past the supermarket. Turn left. Go across the bridge. Then turn right. Go past the school and turn right. The cinema is opposite the school.

☐ Go straight on. Go past the supermarket. Turn left. Go across the bridge. Then turn right. Go past the school and turn left. The cinema is opposite the hospital.

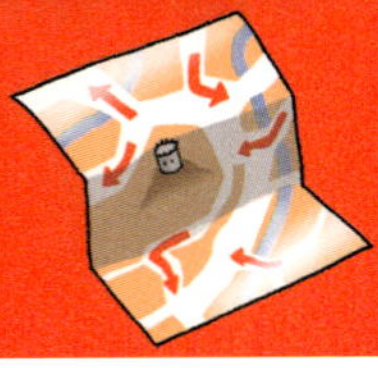

5 Listen and read Clara's e-mail to her class in Austria.

Clara from Austria goes to school in Boston, USA

Dear friends,

I like my new school in Boston. In my class there are 22 children. Our teacher is Mrs Kelly. She is very nice. My best friend is Kim. She is ten years old. I teach Kim German words. She can say "Guten Morgen" and "Tschüss". School begins at nine o'clock. At half past eight I get on the school bus at the corner of our street. I get home at four. Please write soon.

Love,
Clara

This is me.

This is our house.

This is my school.

This is our school bus.

 5 CD 2/13

Culture Special

Here is a photo of Boston.

This is my classroom.

6 **Answer the questions.**

Where is Clara's new school?
How many children are in her class?
What's her teacher's name?
What's her best friend's name?
How old is Kim?
How does Clara get to school?

This is my friend Kim.

7 **Read. Write your own text.**

Where I live

I live in Green Street.
My house is next
to the supermarket.

Where I live

I live in South Street.
My house is number 10.
It's opposite a big park.

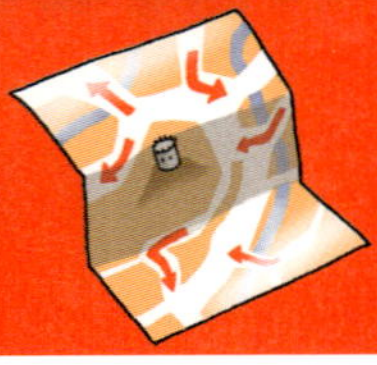

8 Listen. Act out the dialogues.

Dialogue 1:

Tourist: Excuse me, please. Where's the cinema?
Woman: It's on Market Street.
Tourist: Where's that?
Woman: Go straight on. Then turn right at the park.
Tourist: Thank you.

Dialogue 2:

Tourist: Excuse me, where's the supermarket?
Man: OK. Turn left here. Then go across the bridge. You can see the supermarket from the bridge.
Tourist: Thank you very much.
Man: That's OK.

Dialogue 3:

Tourist: Excuse me, please.
Woman: Yes?
Tourist: Where's the zoo?
Woman: Look, there's a bus stop over there.
Tourist: A bus stop?
Woman: Yes, bus 46 takes you to the zoo.
Tourist: Thank you.

8 CD 2/14

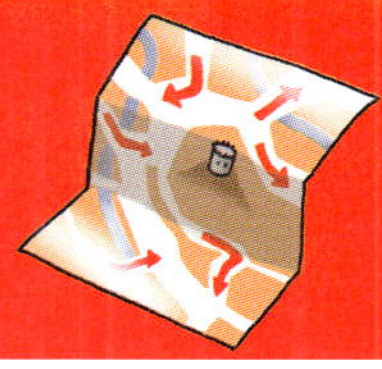

9 **Read and tick *True* or *False* (✔).**

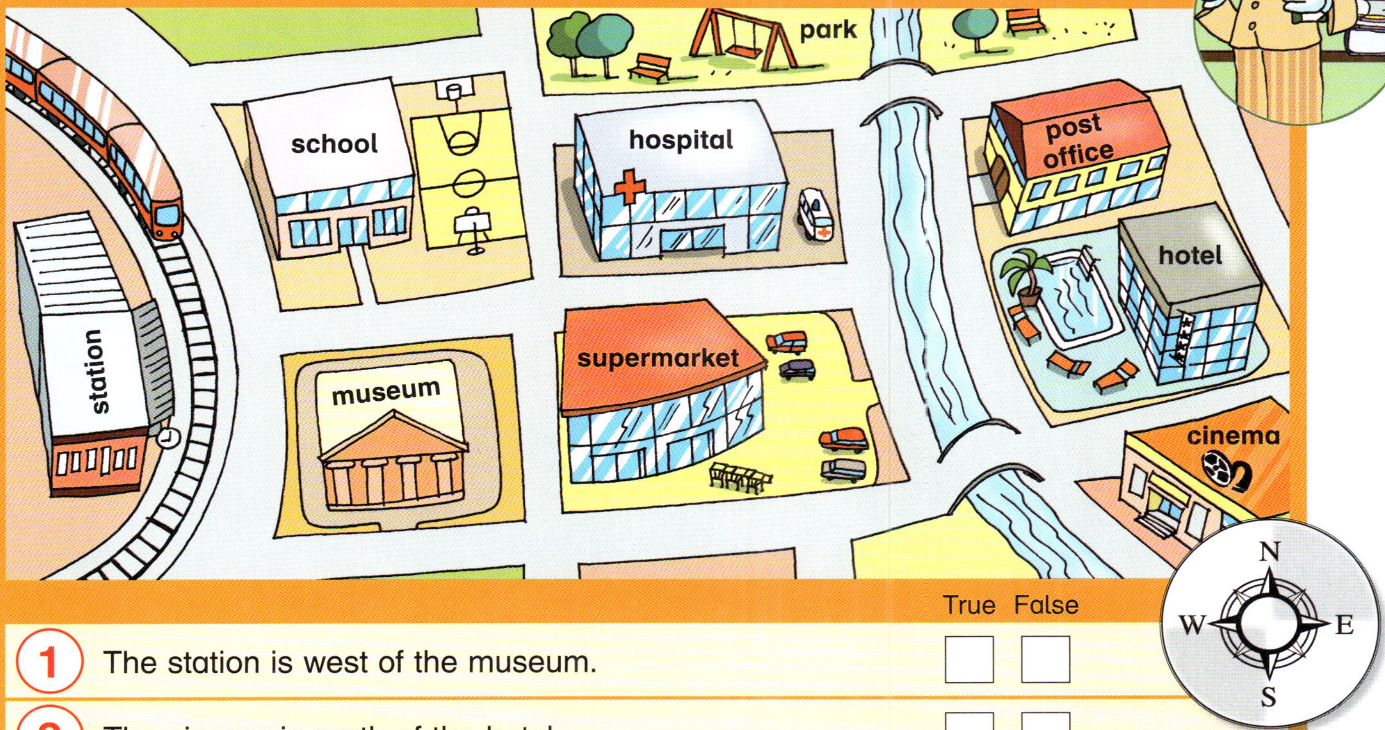

		True	False
1	The station is west of the museum.	☐	☐
2	The cinema is north of the hotel.	☐	☐
3	The school is east of the supermarket.	☐	☐
4	The hotel is south of the post office.	☐	☐
5	The park is west of the post office and the hospital.	☐	☐

10 **Draw and complete.**

1. My house is north of ________________ .
2. ________________ is south of ________________ .
3. ________________ is west of ________________ .
4. ________________ is east of ________________ .

Unit 8 Treasure

1 Listen and find out where the treasure is.

2 Work in pairs. Hide the treasure.

1 CD 2/15

3 Listen. Then write the missing words.

down	across	right	to	left	through	on	up	straight	at	through

Go ____________________ the wood.

Go straight on and then turn ____________________ .

Go ________________ the hill.

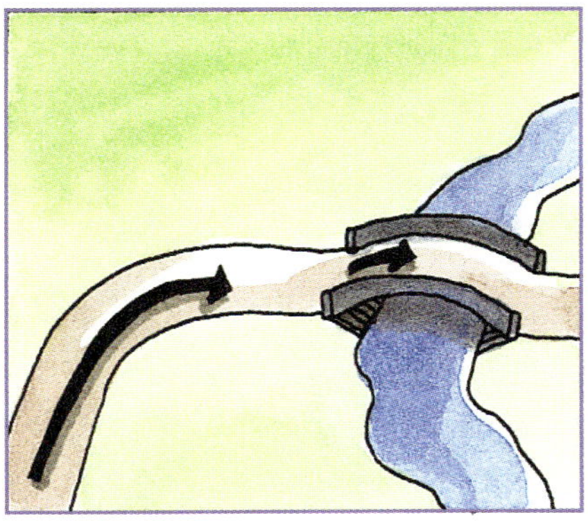

Turn right and go ________________ the bridge.

Go ____________________ the hill.

Go ________________ on.

Turn ____________________ ________________ the farm.

Go straight ________________ and then turn left.

Go ________________ the castle ________________ the wood.

4 **A game. Work in pairs.**

MAP A

MAP B

5 Watch the story. Read and write.

A treasure hunt

I'm scared!	I don't like toffees!
Help me, please!	Go and find the box.

6 Listen and mime. Then listen and point.

The ring

7 Listen and fill in the numbers.

6 CD 2/17 7 CD 2/18

8 Listen to the dialogue. Change it with a partner. Act it out.

Oliver: Look, there's an old box!
Alice: Wow! Let's open it.
Oliver: Maybe there's gold in it.
Alice: Help me open it.
Oliver: OK.
Alice: I don't believe it.
Oliver: What's in it?
Alice: An old shoe!

9 Create a story and act it out. Work with a partner.

10 Read. Write your own text.

My text

In my treasure box there is
a little blue car and my camera.
There are also six beautiful stones.

Holidays

1 Watch the story. Listen and write.

Mr Crocodile and Dr Kangaroo

idea | Next, please. | weeks

1 CD 2/20

asleep hungry finished

2 Listen. Sing the song.

Jungle Party

In the jungle, in the jungle
there's a party tonight.

Arnie the croc
is dancing on a rock.
The hippo in red socks
is swinging with the fox.

The monkey and the cat
are playing with the rat.
The lion and the frog
are singing with the dog.

The mouse and the racoon
have got a blue balloon.
The bird and the snake
are eating all the cake.

3 Listen and fill in the numbers.

4 Listen and read.

I don't like it here

5 Act out the sketch.

4 CD 2/24

6 Watch the story. Read and write.

The school party

We're busy. | Is she the singer? | I'm so sorry. | I don't know.

Units 7-9

Show what you can do

1 **Look, read and fill in the numbers.**

1
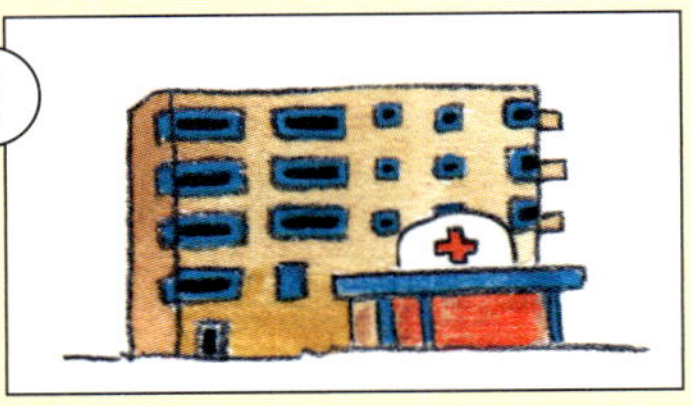

2

3

4

5

6

7

8

9

10

11

12

◯ hill	◯ hospital	◯ broken leg
◯ opposite	◯ wood	◯ go up
◯ guitarist	◯ next to	◯ post office
◯ station	◯ go down	◯ bridge

2 Read the dialogue. Draw the way to the cinema.

3 Fill in *How, What* or *Where.*

 ________________ many children are in your class? –  Twenty-two, I think.

 ________________ does Tom get to school? –  By bus.

 ________________ is in your bag? –  My books.

 ________________ is the supermarket? –  It's opposite the park.

 ________________ is your teacher's name? –  Her name is Mrs Miller.

 ________________ old is your friend? –  He's ten.

Christmas

1 Listen and point.

golden angel

candle

snowman

present

silver bell

golden star

2 Play the game.

1 CD 2/25

3 Listen. Sing the song.

The Christmas tree

Take some silver bells, take a golden star.
Put them on the Christmas tree and sing along with me.
Put them on the Christmas tree and sing along with me.

Join hands and start dancing around the big tree,
and sing "Merry Christmas, Merry Christmas" with me.

Take a little snowman, take some golden angels.
Put them on the Christmas tree and sing along with me.
Put them on the Christmas tree and sing along with me.

Word list

A

angel	Engel
April	April
August	August
aunt	Tante

B

bat	Fledermaus
bad luck	Pech
balloon	Luftballon
beach	Strand
beans	Bohnen
beautiful	wunderschön
believe	glauben
bell	Glocke
best wishes	Liebe Grüße
big	groß
birthday	Geburtstag
box	Kiste
boyfriend	Freund
bridge	Brücke
bring	mitbringen
broken leg	gebrochenes Bein
brother	Bruder
build	bauen
bus stop	Bushaltestelle

C

cake	Kuchen
call	anrufen
camera	Fotoapparat
candle	Kerze
candy floss	Zuckerwatte
castle	Schloss
catch	fangen
cheese	Käse
chicken	Hühnchen, Hendl
chips	Pommes frites
chocolate	Schokolade
cinema	Kino
climb	klettern
coffee	Kaffee
crazy	verrückt
cry	hier: weinen
crybaby	Heulsuse
cupboard (PW2)	Geschirrschrank

D

dad (PW2)	Vater
darling	Liebling
dark	dunkel
daughter	Tochter
December	Dezember
dig	graben
dinosaur	Dinosaurier
Don't be silly.	Sei nicht albern.

E

ears (PW2)	Ohren
elephant (PW1)	Elefant
every	jeden
eyes (PW2)	Augen

F

family (PW2)	Familie
fantastic	fantastisch
fast	schnell
favourite place	Lieblingsplatz/-ort
February	Februar
find	finden
fire brigade	Feuerwehr
fish and chips	Fisch mit Pommes frites
fly	fliegen
food	Essen, Speisen
forget	vergessen
fruit (salad)	Obst(salat)

G

giraffe	Giraffe
go across the bridge	über die Brücke gehen
go down (the hill)	(den Hügel) hinuntergehen
go home	heimgehen
go past (the station)	(am Bahnhof) vorbeigehen
go straight on	geradeaus gehen
go through (the park)	durch (den Park) gehen
go up (the hill)	(den Hügel) hinaufgehen
gold	Gold
grandma	Großmutter
grandpa (PW2)	Großvater
grass	Gras
Great idea!	Super Idee!
guitarist	Gitarrist/in

H

hair (PW2)	Haare
headmistress	Schuldirektorin
high	hoch
hill	Hügel
hippo (PW1)	Nilpferd
hole	Loch
hospital	Krankenhaus
hotel	Hotel
How are you?	Wie geht es dir?
how many	wie viele
hurry	beeilen
hurt	schmerzen, weh tun

J

January	Jänner
July	Juli
jump	springen
June	Juni
jungle	Dschungel

K

kangaroo	Känguru

L

ladies and gentlemen	Damen und Herren
lake	See
land	landen
later	später
laugh	lachen
lay eggs	Eier legen
leg	Bein
lemonade	Zitronenlimonade
leopard	Leopard
(love) letter	(Liebes-)Brief
let's ...	Lass uns ...
library	Bücherei, Bibliothek
lion (PW1)	Löwe
love	lieben

M

map	Karte
March	März
May	Mai
mixed salad	gemischter Salat
money	Geld
monkey (PW1)	Affe
mouth (PW2)	Mund
mum (PW2)	Mutter
museum	Museum
mushroom	Pilz

N

near	nahe
necklace	Kette
Next, please.	Der/Die Nächste bitte.
next to	neben
No way!	Auf keinen Fall!
No problem!	Kein Problem!
November	November

O

oak	Eiche
October	Oktober
of course	sicherlich
often	oft
old	alt
open something	etwas öffnen
opposite	gegenüber
orange juice	Orangensaft
owl	Eule

P

park	Park
peas	Erbsen
penguin	Pinguin
pie	Kuchen
pilot	Pilot
please	bitte
plane (PW1)	Flugzeug
polar bear	Eisbär
post office	Postamt
present (PW1)	Geschenk

R

rat	Ratte
rattlesnake	Klapperschlange
read	lesen
rice	Reis
ring	Ring
river	Fluss
rodeo rider	Rodeoreiter/in

S

sandcastle	Sandburg
sausages	Paar Würstchen
school	Schule
Scotland	Schottland
seagull	Möwe
seal	Seehund
September	September
shark	Hai
shell	Muschel
shy	schüchtern
singer	Sänger/in
sister	Schwester
skate park	Skate Park
sky	Himmel
Sleep well.	Schlaf gut.
small	klein
smile	lächeln
snowman (PW2)	Schneemann
sofa (PW2)	Sofa, Couch
sometimes	manchmal
son	Sohn
Sorry!	Entschuldige/n Sie!
soup	Suppe
spaghetti (PW1)	Spaghetti
spooky	gruselig
star	Stern
station	Bahnhof
supermarket	Supermarkt
surprise	Überraschung
sweet shop	Süßigkeitenladen
swim	schwimmen
swimming pool	Schwimmbad

T

table (PW2)	Tisch
tea	Tee
teacher	Lehrer/in
teeth (PW2)	Zähne
thief	Dieb
today	heute
toffee	Karamellbonbon
treasure	Schatz
tree (house)	Baum(haus)
try	versuchen
turn left	links abbiegen
turn right	rechts abbiegen

U

uncle	Onkel
useful	nützlich

W

walk	gehen, spazieren
want	möchten
watch TV	fernsehen
weather	Wetter
We're busy.	Wir sind beschäftigt.
weekend	Wochenende
whale	Wal
What's the matter?/ What's wrong?	Was ist los?
Where's ...?	Wo ist ...?
Who is ...?	Wer ist ...?
wish	Wunsch
wonderful	wunderbar
wood	Wald

Y

Yes, of course.	Ja, selbstverständlich.

Z

zoo	Zoo

PLAYWAY

Elterninformation

Liebe Eltern, so funktioniert Englischlernen mit *PLAYWAY*

◆ Ihr Kind lernt
- die Bedeutung und Schreibweise englischer Wörter mit Hilfe von ***Picture Cards*** und ***Word Cards***.
- die Aussprache neuer Wörter mit Hilfe von Liedern und Reimen von einer **Audio-CD**.
- lustige Sketches und Geschichten durch Videosequenzen auf **DVD** zu verstehen.
- einfache Dialoge auf Englisch zu führen.

ISBN 978-3-85061-722-2
Preis: € 39,90

Spaß am Nachmittag oder Wochenende gibt es bei PLAYWAY natürlich auch.

PLAYWAY – Die CD-ROM für zu Hause

Mit der interaktiven und multimedialen Englisch-Training-Software geht's auf in die virtuelle Welt von Max und seinen Freunden, die alle in einer ganz besonderen Straße im *PLAYWAY*-Land leben: der Lern- und Spielstraße.
Hier gibt es die unterschiedlichsten Stationen, an denen die Kinder ihre Englischkenntnisse auf den Prüfstand stellen können. Klar, dass Max immer hilft, wenn's mal klemmt.

Die CD-ROM bietet:
- mehr als 20 Stunden Übungsmaterial
- 15 Übungstypen mit 25 Varianten
- ca. 45 Minuten voll animierte *Cartoons*
- Karaoke Funktion für *Songs* und *Chants*
- ein mitwachsendes *Dictionary*
- einen kapitelweisen Aufbau für einen einfachen Zugriff.

Systemvoraussetzungen:
Betriebssysteme: Windows 2000, XP, Vista, Win7; Prozessor: Pentium/Celeron/Athlon/Thunderbird, mind. 1000 MHz; Arbeitsspeicher: Unter Win 2000, Win XP: mind. 256 MB, Vista, Win7: 1024 MB Freier Speicherplatz auf der Festplatte: mind. 800 MB; CD-ROM Laufwerk/Soundkarte; Grafikkarte: mind. 16 Bit Farbe (High Color)

Infos und Prospekte direkt bei

HELBLING
Verlagsgesellschaft m.b.H.
Kaplanstraße 9
Postfach 12
A-6063 Rum
Tel. 0512/262333-0
Fax 0512/262333-111

E-Mail:
office@helbling.co.at

Homepage:
www.helbling.at

Helbling

Bestellkarte für *Kinder*, Eltern und Lehrer!

Stück	Titel	Preis
	 **PLAYWAY 4 CD-ROM** 978-3-85061-722-2 Multimediales Englisch-Training mit Max CD-ROM mit umfangreichem Booklet	**€ 39,90**

Datum

Unterschrift (Bei Minderjährigen die/der Erziehungsberechtigte)

Die Lieferung erfolgt auf Rechnung zuzüglich Portokosten. Unverbindliche Preisempfehlung.
Preise freibleibend, Stand 1.11.2011; Änderungen vorbehalten.

PLAYWAY

Spielerisch Lernen – mit System

EINFACH ZU BESTELLEN!
Die beiliegende Bestellkarte zum Ausschneiden einfach in einer Buchhandlung abgeben oder an folgende Adresse senden:

➜ *www.helbling.at*

HELBLING Verlagsgesellschaft m.b.H.
A-6063 RUM · Kaplanstraße 9 · Postfach 12
Tel. 0512/262333-0 · Fax 0512/262333-111

Sie können auch via Internet bestellen.

Unsere E-Mail-Adresse lautet:
office@helbling.co.at

oder Sie besuchen unsere Homepage.
Hier finden Sie, neben unserem Bestellservice und der umfangreichen Produktinfo, auch viele interessante Anregungen und Tipps für Eltern und Kids:

www.helbling.at

Absender:
(Bitte in Blockschrift!)

E-Mail:

Vorname Familienname

Straße

Postleitzahl Ort

Schule (Name und Ort)

Antwort

An

HELBLING
Verlagsgesellschaft m.b.H.

Kaplanstraße 9 · Postfach 12
A-6063 RUM